AN ODE TO LIFE

In realms where life and death entwine,
I ponder existence, the divine.
For my joy to bloom, others must pay,
Such truths we face, yesterday and today.

Before I judge, before stones cast,
Let me seek humility, my soul's glass.
Aware of my role in this cosmic dance,
Compassion's stance, my heart's advance.

Not for dominance or selfish gain,
But to ease pain, my life's refrain.
A humble prayer, deep in my core,
May my footprints bring goodness ashore.

Love and compassion, a beacon to start,
An artful work, a hopeful heart.
Oh, envision a life adorned with grace,
Smiles on every face, in love's embrace.

Illustrations by Craiyon
Cover image by rawpixel.com on Freepik
Design by Liliana Guia

ISBN 979-8-9898889-0-0 (ebook)
ISBN 979-8-9898889-1-7 (hardcover)
ISBN 979-8-9898889-2-4 (paperback)

billybunterhimalayan@gmail.com

Boond

For Surakshit-ji.

My teacher and friend, whose wisdom and compassion have been an invaluable blessing on my life's journey. May everyone be blessed with such a guiding light on their path through life.

I am truly grateful to Alex Wynter – your intuition, insights and patient support took a rough diamond and allowed it to sparkle. And a big thank you to Sama and Craiyon... for quietly holding my hand through this whole process.

Billy Bunter, the Himalayan

Boond

The Original...
Zero, zero, zero
A nobody.
With nothing.
In shunya.

Contents

CONTENTS

An Ocean Encounter

ONE WARM SUMMER DAY, BOOND, A spirited droplet, found himself floating on the surface of the Indian Ocean, relishing the gentle cradling caused by the ebb and flow of the tide. Bathed in the golden hues of the sun, Boond basked in the shimmering dance of light upon the water. The ocean stretched out as far as the eye could see, a vast expanse of mystery and wonder. It was a world teeming with life, from the colorful corals swaying beneath the surface to the graceful movements of marine creatures.

But his tranquility was abruptly interrupted when, with a whimsical "poof," Boond vanished into thin air, quite literally! The sun's warmth embraced the tiny droplet, transforming him into an invisible vapor that rose skyward. With a newfound sense of freedom, Boond bid farewell to his watery home, embarking on an extraordinary adventure beyond the confines of the ocean.

The Skyward Gathering

IN THE VAST EXPANSE OF THE sky, Boond, now airborne, joined the company of countless other droplets. Amongst the billowing clouds, they formed a congregation of dreams and aspirations, suspended in the boundless azure. The atmosphere embraced them, carrying them on a gentle breeze that whispered tales of distant lands and untold wonders.

For a while, they gazed down upon the Earth below, beholding the magnificent blue waters of the ocean that had been their home. The rhythmic waves, like a lullaby, echoed in their collective memory, evoking a sense of longing and nostalgia. As the winds playfully guided them northeast, they embarked on a grand adventure, witnessing the tapestry of the land unfold beneath them.

It was during this wondrous journey that Boond struck up a conversation with two fellow droplets, each with their own unique personality.

"Hello there," Boond exclaimed with a twinkle in his watery eye, "I am Boond. The Original Boond. Triple O zero. Pleasure to make your acquaintance!"

Sip, a lively droplet with a mischievous sparkle, greeted Boond with a playful gleam in her liquid eyes. "Well, hello, Boond! Fancy meeting a droplet with such an intriguing name. I'm Sip. Just Sip," she exclaimed with a hint of mischief.

Ripple, a more serene and contemplative droplet, smiled warmly and added, "And I'm Ripple, delighted to join in this enchanting conversation. Welcome to our journey, Boond."

Their companionship blossomed amidst the vastness of the sky, as they shared stories of their aquatic origins and marveled at the wonders that awaited them.

The Enchanting Ascent

GUIDED BY THE CURRENTS OF THE wind, Boond, Ripple, and Sip soared over the vast landscapes of the Indian subcontinent. As they left the shores of India behind, they marveled at the breathtaking scenery below. The verdant Western Ghats unfurled like an emerald carpet, their lush forests and cascading waterfalls captivating their gaze. The vibrant hues of nature painted a picturesque backdrop, bewitching them with the diversity and beauty of the land.

Drifting farther north, they witnessed a transformation in the terrain. The arid landscapes of Rajasthan emerged, painted in earthy tones and adorned with majestic sand dunes that seemed to ripple like waves frozen in time.

As they ventured onward, passing over the arid plains, the winds carried them to the northern regions of Haryana and Punjab. The fertile plains of western India stretched out before them, adorned with yellow fields of wheat and mustard blooms creating a patchwork quilt below, a testament to the agricultural heartland of the country. The scent of the soil and the sight of hardworking farmers tending to their crops filled the air, infusing Boond, Ripple, and Sip with a sense of reverence for the land and its people.

Finally, after their remarkable journey across diverse landscapes, the trio reached the foothills of the mighty Himalayas. The snow-capped peaks rose imposingly before them, reaching towards the heavens. The air grew ever crisper, and the silence became profound as they ventured deeper into the heart of the mountains.

Amidst the rugged beauty and grandeur of the Himalayas, Boond, Ripple, and Sip felt a sense of awe and humility. The towering peaks seemed to beckon them, their jagged edges tracing an invisible path that led to the highest realms of the world. Anticipation grew as they prepared for the final leg of their ascent, ready to discover the mysteries hidden amidst the snow-clad summits.

With each passing moment, their ascent filled them with a sense of wonder and anticipation. The land they had traversed, the diverse terrains they had witnessed, and the people and creatures they had encountered along the way had enriched their journey.

Quite suddenly, a weight enveloped them, as if the mountains themselves gently placed their touch upon the intrepid droplets. In a fascinating metamorphosis, Boond, Sip, and Ripple transformed into exquisite, pristine bodies of white. They marveled at their newfound beauty; their transparency now replaced by a snowy brilliance that sparkled in the sunlight.

A Whimsical Ballet

AS THE SNOWFLAKES DESCENDED, THE ATMOSPHERE around them came alive with swirling snowfall. The winds became their playful companions, guiding them through a lighthearted dance in the air. They rode the eddies and currents, feeling as though they were on a celestial roller coaster, their crystalline bodies glistening and sparkling under the wintry sky.

The air was filled with a delicate symphony of whispers as the snowflakes brushed against each other. Their graceful movements resembled the fluttering of wings, carrying them closer to the awaiting Earth. The three friends marveled at the fascinating sight unfolding below them.

As they descended further, the landscape began to reveal itself. They caught glimpses of towering trees adorned with a delicate lacework of snow, their branches reaching out like welcoming arms. The brushes and shrubs below seemed to sway with anticipation, as if bowing in reverence to their imminent arrival.

The closer they came to the Earth's embrace, the more details emerged. They could discern the intricate patterns of frost on windows, the rooftops blanketed in white, and the soft undulations of untouched meadows. The landscape became a canvas painted with shades of purity and tranquility, offering solace and a sense of belonging.

In the midst of this ethereal descent, a flash of movement caught their attention. A magnificent Himalayan leopard gracefully leaped through the snow-covered terrain, its spotted coat blending seamlessly with the wintry landscape. Its eyes met theirs for a fleeting moment, and the snowflakes became a part of the wild beauty of the Himalayas.

As the friends floated downward, they reveled in the collective beauty surrounding them. They were but tiny fragments of a larger masterpiece, an intricate mosaic woven by nature's hand. Their laughter echoed through the silent air, accompanied by the tinkling sound of millions of snowflakes touching down upon the Earth's surface.

Together, they continued their whimsical ballet, their movements growing gentler as they approached their final destination. With each passing moment, the anticipation built, for they were about to complete their remarkable journey and embark on a new chapter in their frozen existence.

Blanketed in Silence

As Boond, Sip, and Ripple gently touched the Earth's surface, they did something quite extraordinary. They intertwined their crystalline hands, determined to stay together amidst the vastness of the snowy expanse. Hand in hand, they glided gracefully, leaving behind delicate imprints upon the snowy canvas.

The snowflakes around them seemed to welcome their arrival, as if embracing them into the fold of their sparkling community. They were surrounded by countless others, each unique in their design, coming together in a harmonious ensemble of frozen beauty. The air was filled with a profound silence, broken only by the whispering caress of snowflakes falling from the heavens.

As the day slowly waned, the soft glow of sunlight began to fade, casting a warm, amber hue upon the landscape. The transition from light to dusk painted the sky with hues of oranges and pinks, creating a breathtaking tableau. Boond, Sip, and Ripple felt a sense of awe and wonder, as if they were witnessing nature's own masterpiece unfold before their crystalline eyes.

Gradually, darkness enveloped the world, and the stars began to twinkle in the velvety night sky. The moon, a silver orb suspended in the heavens, cast a gentle glow upon the snowy terrain. It was a realm of shadows and mystery, where the snowflakes found solace in the depths of the night.

But there was another darkness, a different kind that awaited them. As they settled upon the Earth's surface, the falling snowflakes above continued to descend, layer upon layer, adding depth and weight to the snowy landscape. Fresh snowflakes embraced Boond, Sip, and Ripple, covering them with a pristine white veil.

This additional layer of snow brought a cocooning embrace that shielded them from the outside world. They could feel the weight of the snow pressing upon them, a gentle pressure that anchored them to the Earth. They were enveloped in a darkness that brought a sense of safety and stillness, as if they were cradled within nature's tender arms.

Buried beneath the weight of their fellow flakes, Boond, Sip, and Ripple experienced a slow metamorphosis. The lightness of their descent gradually gave way to a sense of being nestled and protected. Layer upon layer of snow embraced them, shielding them from the outside world. They became part of a tapestry woven by millions of snowflakes, creating a unified blanket of serenity.

Time seemed to stand still as the snowflakes settled, and the world became a profoundly quiet and soothing sanctuary. The snowfall continued, filling the landscape with a sense of purity and magic.

Together, they held hands, their crystalline fingers interwoven, finding comfort and strength in their unity. They whispered tales of their journey, sharing their hopes, dreams, and aspirations. The darkness embraced them, becoming a canvas upon which they could paint their shimmering thoughts and emotions.

As the night deepened, the world slumbered beneath a snowy embrace. Boond, Sip, and Ripple, nestled within the bosom of the Earth, drifted into a deep sleep. They became part of the silence, their consciousness blending with the wintery landscape, as the night unfolded its mysteries, and the world awaited the dawn of a new day.

Slumber in
Winter's Embrace

WRAPPED IN THE GENTLE EMBRACE OF the majestic mountain's icy grip, Boond, Sip, and Ripple surrendered to a deep slumber. They drifted into a realm of dreams, their delicate forms merging with the hibernating landscape. Time seemed to slip away, as the outside world embarked on its journey through the seasons, oblivious to the placid tableau beneath the snow.

Winter arrived, its frigid breath casting a deep stillness upon the land. The earth lay dormant, cocooned in a blanket of snow, while frost painted delicate patterns on every surface. The days grew shorter, the nights longer, and the air carried a crispness that whispered of silent dreams. Boond, Sip, and Ripple, nestled beneath layers of white, experienced the world's slumber alongside their own.

With the arrival of spring, the land awakened from its dormancy. The sun's warmth kissed the earth, coaxing delicate shoots to push through the thawing soil. Nature's brushstrokes painted the landscape with vibrant colors, as blossoms burst forth in a concerto of scents and hues. Birds returned from their distant migrations, serenading the awakening world with melodies of hope and rebirth. Yet, Boond, Sip, and Ripple remained immersed in their peaceful sleep, untouched by the joyous revival outside.

Spring blossomed into summer, and the world shimmered under the radiant embrace of the sun. Days grew longer, basking the land in a brilliant glow. Vibrant meadows swayed in the gentle breeze, offering a kaleidoscope of wildflowers that danced to the rhythm of life. Bees hummed in harmonious delight, while butterflies painted the air with their delicate wings. Yet, the three slumbering snowflakes remained oblivious to the lively symphony of the summer season.

And so, through the cycle of seasons, winter led to spring, and spring gave way to the verdant green of summer. Boond, Sip, and Ripple remained cocooned within their sanctuary, undisturbed by the ebb and flow of time, awaiting the moment when they would awaken once more.

The Dance
of Awakening

BOOND, SIP, AND RIPPLE STIRRED FROM their deep slumber, awakening to a world transformed. The gentle warmth of the sun finally kissed their delicate forms, infusing them with renewed energy and purpose. It was then they realized that a considerable span of time had passed—a full nine months of hibernation.

Stretching their fluid bodies, the friends marveled at the subtle changes they had undergone. Once pristine snowflakes, they had transformed into shimmering droplets, each containing the spirit of their journey. The three companions embraced their new forms with delight, for they were now poised to embark on a thrilling adventure down the mountainside.

With hearts brimming with joy, they danced and skipped their way along the glistening slopes, their tiny surfaces sparkling in the sunlight. Their laughter mingled with the bubbling melodies of nearby brooks, as they joyously joined the flow of water. The brooks grew in strength, merging with countless other streams and tributaries, forming a network of rushing currents that surged through the mountains.

As they journeyed, Boond, Sip, and Ripple passed through verdant meadows adorned with an array of captivating flowers. Delicate rhododendrons painted the landscape with hues of crimson and pink, while cheerful daisies danced in the meadow breeze. Bright blue Himalayan poppies and fragrant wildflowers added their vibrant presence to the rich assortment of colors. The air was infused with the sweet scent of jasmine and lavender, blending with the earthy fragrance of the Himalayan soil.

Amidst this riot of colors and scents, Boond, Sip, and Ripple reveled in the beauty surrounding them. They delighted in the camaraderie of fellow droplets, forging deep and meaningful connections as they traveled together. They met Raina, a spirited sphere with a playful nature, and Misty, a gentle mist that danced alongside them, weaving intricate patterns in the air. Each encounter enriched their journey, as they exchanged stories, shared laughter, and formed unbreakable bonds.

Together, they continued their downstream journey, their newfound friendships adding depth and meaning to their collective adventure.

The Roar of the Mighty River

FOR TWO DAYS, BOOND AND HIS cohort of friends traveled joyfully, their laughter echoing through the air as they sped along the river's course. The sun dipped below the horizon, casting a dusky hue over the landscape, signaling the onset of night. It was then that they heard it—a distant, ominous roar that reverberated through the stillness of the night.

With each passing hour, the roar grew louder, casting a shadow of unease upon their hearts. Ripple and Raina huddled close together, seeking solace in their shared fears. Boond, determined to lift their spirits, mustered all his courage and began to sing a melodious gurgle song, his voice echoing through the darkness. But the joy that once permeated their journey had now been replaced by a sense of foreboding.

As the hours ticked by, their pace quickened, propelled forward by an invisible force. They turned around a bend, and suddenly, before their eyes, lay the largest river they had ever beheld. The roar now deafening, they could barely comprehend the sheer magnitude of the rushing waters. It seemed as if millions of droplets were falling from the very skies itself, cascading down in a terrifying display of chaos and frenzy.

Fear gripped Boond, Sip, Ripple, Misty, and Raina as they clung to one another, their bodies hurtling uncontrollably towards the edge of the seething waterfall. Tossed and turned amidst the torrent, their cries merged with the collective screams of their fellow droplets, each one seemingly destined for their demise. Down they plummeted, surrendering to the unknown, their voices lost amidst the deafening tumult.

Their descent was fraught with chaos and disarray, their bodies colliding with the unyielding force of a boulder lurking in the darkness. The impact sent them spiraling into a realm of obscurity, where light surrendered to shadow. Darkness enveloped them, their consciousness fading into a void of dark uncertainty.

Lost in the River's Embrace

BOND'S EYES FLUTTERED OPEN, HIS AWARENESS slowly emerging from the depths of unconsciousness. He blinked, trying to clear the haze that clouded his vision. A searing pain pulsated through every aspect of his liquid essence, a persistent reminder of the tumultuous descent they had endured. Groggily, he looked around, seeking familiar faces amidst the swirling chaos.

His gaze fell upon Sip, Raina, and Misty, their droplet forms clustered together, their expressions mirroring his own confusion and pain. Ripple, however, was conspicuously absent. Panic gripped Boond's heart as he realized the absence of their dear companion. A shiver ran through him, and his voice quivered as he shook Sip, Raina, and Misty, desperately calling out to them.

"Have you seen Ripple?" Boond's voice trembled with a mixture of fear and urgency. As his companions stirred, their eyes filled with worry, the weight of Ripple's absence settling heavily upon them. The vastness of the river that surrounded them was overwhelming, a stark contrast to the intimate brook they once called home. They felt like minuscule droplets lost in an endless expanse of water.

Driven by a shared sense of loss, they frantically searched, their droplet bodies fanning out in all directions. Boond's heart pounded as he scoured the swirling currents, desperately hoping for a glimpse of Ripple's familiar form. But no matter how fervently they searched, Ripple remained elusive, swallowed by the vastness of the river's flow.

Exhausted and disheartened, the four friends regrouped, their bodies aching from the physical toll of their journey and the emotional weight of their missing companion. They formed a tight-knit circle, their droplet forms trembling with a mixture of grief and resolve. In the face of adversity, they drew strength from each other, their unyielding bond a beacon of hope in the darkness that surrounded them.

As they continued their descent down the mighty Sutlej River, they merged with countless other droplets, becoming a collective speck in the vast expanse of water. Their individual identities blurred, they embraced the oneness of their journey, their shared destiny driving them forward. The river carried them with its unstoppable current, their future uncertain, trying to keep their spirits resilient.

In the depths of the night, as the river whispered its secrets and the moon cast its heavenly glow upon the waters, Boond, Sip, Raina, and Misty pressed onward. They clung to the memories of Ripple; their hearts heavy with loss but fueled by the flickering hope of a reunion. With each passing moment, they vowed to persevere, to navigate the treacherous currents and find their way back to the light.

And so, they drifted, a small collective of droplets bound by an unbreakable bond, forging ahead into the unknown. In their unity, they found solace, drawing strength from their friendship. With each passing eddy and every twist and turn of the river's course, they carried Ripple's spirit within them, never losing sight of the love that bound them together.

Boond's Freedom

IN THE DEPTHS OF HIS SORROW, Boond found himself grappling with the relentless grip of grief. While he maintained a facade of composure among his friends, his thoughts were consumed by Ripple. In the midst of laughter and conversations, he would infiltrate his consciousness, casting a shadow of despair upon his heart. Even when surrounded by the breathtaking beauty of snow-capped mountains and lush green meadows, memories of Ripple would seize him, plunging him into a sea of longing.

Gradually, Boond became aware of the profound impact of attachment on his well-being and his ability to truly live in the present. He observed the ebb and flow of his emotions, how they swung between fleeting moments of happiness and depths of desolation when his mind drifted into the past. He began to discern that attachment was nothing more than a continuous rehashing of what had been, a persistent source of his sorrow.

In the face of this realization, Boond started to comprehend the futility of resisting the natural order of life, the inevitability of change, gain, and loss. He saw the impermanence that colored every aspect of existence, the transient nature of all experiences and relationships. This understanding stirred within him a desire for liberation from the chains of attachment.

With steadfastness, Boond sought to quiet his restless mind, refusing to let it drag him back into the clutches of the past. He recognized the power of redirecting his focus to the present moment, to the vibrant tapestry of sights, sounds, and sensations that surrounded him.

He embraced the aliveness of the present, finding solace in the new landscapes, conversations, and friendships that unfolded before him. The snow-capped mountains towered before him, their stately peaks piercing the heavens, glistening like diamonds in the embrace of the sun's gentle caress. Each crevice and ridge whispered stories of resilience and strength, a testament to the enduring spirit of nature.

The air carried an ensemble of scents, a melange of fragrances that stirred his soul. The sweet aroma of wildflowers danced on the breeze, mingling with the earthy scent of the Himalayan soil. Jasmine and lavender, delicate and intoxicating, perfumed the air, their sublime spirit igniting a sense of wonder within Boond. He breathed deeply, inhaling the essence of whatever wafted by him, letting it fill every bit of his being.

Amidst this grand panorama of nature, Boond reveled in the conversations that unfolded around him. He listened intently to the tales shared by fellow droplets, each one a fragment of a larger story. The laughter of merging brooks, cascading over rocks in playful abandon, echoed through the valleys, their joy contagious. They hinted at secrets of hidden realms and enchanted forests, inviting Boond to explore the mysteries that lay beyond.

He encountered goats, nimble and sure-footed, gracefully traversing the mountainside. Their coats, a patchwork of brown and white, blended seamlessly with the rugged landscape. Their bleats harmonized with the rustling of leaves and the murmurs of the river, creating a symphony of nature's orchestra. Boond watched in awe as they danced across the rocky terrain, seemingly defying gravity with each nimble leap.

With every passing moment, Boond drank in the beauty that surrounded him, immersing himself in the vivid tapestry of life. He marveled at the interplay of light and shadow, as the sun's ochre rays painted the landscape in a mosaic of colors. He watched as droplets from nearby streams joined the river's flow, their paths converging to create a magnificent unity, an ever-changing mosaic of existence.

And in the midst of this kaleidoscope, Boond felt his own Self, his own aliveness, more vivid than ever before. The past no longer held him captive; it had become a treasured part of his journey, woven into the fabric of his being. He embraced the freedom that came with being fully present, with savoring every moment as if it were a fleeting masterpiece of nature's art.

In this newfound state of awareness, Boond actually experienced the freedom of detachment. He no longer allowed his mind to hijack his attention, pulling him away from the richness of the present.

With an open heart and a mind liberated from the shackles of attachment, Boond embarked on a new chapter of his journey down the Sutlej River. He embraced the harmony of sights and scents, the conversations and connections that enriched his life. And as he flowed with the river's currents, he carried within him the wisdom of Presence, ready to seize each moment as a precious gift, cherishing the beauty that unfolded with every heartbeat.

The Morning Rituals of Pontiffa

In the village of Rupayan, nestled high up in the majestic Himalayas, there stood a revered temple that held a profound significance for the local community. The temple, adorned with intricate carvings and colorful flags, stood as a beacon of spirituality and devotion. At its heart resided Pontiffa, the octogenarian priest whose wisdom and gentle demeanor commanded deep respect.

As the first rays of the morning sun painted the sky with gilded hues, Pontiffa embarked on his daily routine. Ablutions performed with meticulous care, he purified his body and mind, preparing himself for the divine communion that awaited him within the temple walls. With hands clasped in prayer, he chanted ancient hymns, their sacred verses resonating through the tranquil air.

After completing the prayers, Pontiffa adorned his forehead with a vibrant red tikka, symbolizing devotion and divine blessings. The rich fragrance of incense filled the temple, mingling with the gentle aroma of fresh flowers placed as offerings to the gods. The atmosphere hummed with reverence and spirituality, creating an otherworldly ambiance that enveloped both the priest and the temple.

Leaving the sanctuary of the temple, Pontiffa began his descent towards the river, a path etched into the mountainside by generations past. The winding trail, cobble stones in some sections, raw mud in others, meandered through emerald meadows, where wildflowers swayed in harmony with the whispering breeze.

The towering Himalayan peaks stood like sentinels, their snow-capped majesty reflecting the golden glow of the sun. The rhythmic melody of distant waterfalls mingled with the concerto of birdcalls, filled Pontiffa's heart with a sense of elation which never seemed to age. The path, lined with ancient trees and vibrant shrubs, led Pontiffa towards the life-giving Sutlej River, its crystal-clear waters cascading over smooth rocks.

With a serene grace, Pontiffa reached the river's edge, the cool touch of the water soothing his feet. He immersed the copper container – lotah – in the pristine currents, watching as the water swirled and danced within the vessel. This water, the lifeblood of the village, would soon be used in the

sacred abhishek, an offering to the deities that would bless the community with abundance and protection.

Pontiffa filled the sacramental lotah. The interplay of sunlight and shadows on the river's surface, the murmur of the flowing water, and the panoramic vista of mountains and meadows painted a masterpiece of nature's artistry. It was in this spiritual communion with the elements that Pontiffa felt the interconnectedness of all life.

With the lotah filled and his heart brimming with gratitude, Pontiffa retraced his steps along the path, his mind tranquil and his soul nourished. The village of Rupayan awaited, its streets alive with anticipation for the rituals that would unite the community in devotion and celebration.

A Dance of
Flight and Despair

IN THE SOOTHING EMBRACE OF THE early morning, as the sun's amber tendrils dissolved the lingering mist along the riverbanks, Boond, Raina, and Misty engaged in lively conversation, their laughter and banter harmonizing with the rhythmic flow of the Sutlej. But amidst their camaraderie, a figure emerged, a droplet of unparalleled grace. Sip, with fiery determination in her core, embarked on a dance of dreams, an orchestration of acrobatics that transcended the realm of water.

With a deep breath, Sip summoned her very soul, gathering momentum like a swirling tempest. Launching herself into the air, she defied gravity's grasp, ascending higher and higher, her liquid form radiating with transcendent splendor. In those suspended moments, she transformed into an iridescent speck, a celestial creature soaring towards the heavens. As she reached the apex of her arc, time itself seemed to pause, holding its breath in awe of her audacity.

Then, like a brushstroke across the canvas of the sky, Sip flattened herself, stretching her glistening surface into a slender plane. Gliding through the air, she reveled in the exhilaration of flight, an eagle in the body of a droplet. Time seemed to suspend as she traversed the very heavens, suspended in a realm between earth and sky.

Gravity tugged at Sip constantly, the force of nature threatening to pull her down into the rushing waters below. Fear intertwined with resoluteness as she defied the instinct to retreat. With unwavering resolve, she summoned her courage, refusing to succumb to the fear that whispered to her, holding her pancake form for one, just one additional second. In that precarious dance between bravery and trepidation, Sip elongated herself in that final moment, piercing the surface of the river with the precision of an arrow, her form melding with the currents.

The murmurs of the river's other inhabitants swelled into a chorus of wonder, their admiration echoing through the depths of the Sutlej. Sip's acrobatic displays had become a captivating spectacle, a ballet of liquid grace that entranced both droplets and nature itself.

Refusing to rest on her laurels, Sip emerged from the depths, her spirit resolute and unyielding. Without a moment's pause, she gathered herself, ready to embark on the audacious quest once again. Higher she leaped, suspended in the air, her ephemeral wings catching the sunlight. Time seemed to hold its breath as she defied the limits of her liquid existence, striving to reach new heights. There were moments when she met the water with a painful crash, but undeterred, she rose, fueled by a resolve that burned brighter than the sun itself.

Sip was determined to soar to levels that no other droplet had ever reached.

Again and again, she would take flight, each time trying to reach higher.

Further.

But alas, the whims of fate are capricious, and on one of her mightiest flights, the tranquility shattered. A sudden gust of wind, an unforeseen intruder, violently veered Sip off her intended course. She was propelled sideways, hurtling towards a treacherous collision with a merciless rock, an unforgiving sentinel of the riverbank. The onlookers, Boond, Raina, and Misty could only bear witness to this cruel twist of destiny, their hearts gripped with a sense of helplessness.

In a swift response, driven by love and friendship, Boond, Raina, and Misty dove deep beneath the tumultuous surface, so they could swim as quickly as possible. Their liquid forms weaved through the eddies, fear and adrenaline rushing through them until they reached their fragile friend. With delicate tenderness, they enveloped Sip, whose spirit had been momentarily dimmed by the harsh encounter with the unyielding stone. With loving devotion, they guided their path along the placid riverbank, where the waters whispered soothing melodies.

In their watery sanctuary, they cradled Sip like a precious jewel. The gentle currents carried them along, their path guided by an innate understanding of the healing power of solace. Melodies of wisdom flowed through the waters, murmuring reassurance that rippled through their essence. The river itself became their confidant.

Boond, Raina, and Misty formed a protective shield around Sip, their collective strength a confirmation of their unwavering loyalty. They infused her wounded spirit with their own resilience, channeling their devotion to rekindle the flickering life within her as their fluid arrangement carried her along.

With each passing moment, Sip's spirit grew stronger, fueled by the unconditional love of her loyal companions. The healing powers of their friendship transformed her from a broken droplet into a beacon of resilience and hope. In the gentle flow of the currents, they nurtured her, reminding her of her own strength and fortitude.

Yet, unbeknownst to them all, a foreboding presence loomed over- head. An ominous shadow gradually enshrouded the sun, casting a veil of darkness upon the river's edge. Unseen and unheard, a hard cop- per container materialized, sinking into the depths, summoning them toward an uncertain fate. Turmoil ensued, a tempest of confusion and chaos, as the droplets were swept away, drawn into the jaws of a water- fall. Enclosed within the metallic confines, they had become captives, trapped amidst countless others, their voices muted by the echoes of their sudden imprisonment. No longer were they held in the embrace of their home, the Sutlej. The gurgle of the river seemed to get fainter by the minute, replaced by the haunting hush of captivity. Within their hearts, an icy darkness settled, suspended in an uncertain future.

The Abhishek

WITHIN THE CONFINEMENTS OF THE COPPER lotah, the four friends huddled together, their tiny forms enveloped in darkness. They felt like lost souls trapped in a deep, foreboding dungeon, circling the lotah's walls, in search of an elusive escape.

Amidst the darkness, reverberations of an unfamiliar language echoed through the chamber. The giant who had captured them unleashed indecipherable intonations, interwoven with the sacred chant of the universe – OM.

The Unstruck Sound, the primordial Word, the Universal Vibration.

Confusion and terror gripped their beings, but within that fear, they clung to the only familiar sound that offered solace – the resonance of OM, somewhere deep within, a faint memory and a source of peace.

After what felt like an eternity, the chanting ceased abruptly, leaving silence in its wake. The lotah, lifted with a violent force, jolted the friends together, causing their fragile forms to collide with one another and the lotah's inner surface. Slowly, the vessel began to tilt, its angle steepening with each passing moment. Then, without warning, all the droplets were launched into the air, caught in a chaotic dance of free-fall. Their bodies careened through space, crashing against a stone statue of a beaming figure holding a flute—a sculpture exuding a joyful energy that echoed the words, "Hare Krishna... Hare Krishna," filling the air.

As the droplets cascaded down the statue's surface, they mingled with a different breed of droplets, distinct from their translucent bodies. These strangers were larger, heavier, and radiated a pristine milky whiteness. The encounter added yet another layer of confusion to their already bewildered state. Over time, all the droplets trickled down a deep furrow at the base of the statue, before dripping down a copper pipe.

Gradually, all the droplets, both Translucent and Milky White, found themselves crowded together once more, now confined within a much larger container—a vessel that dwarfed the one they had been unceremoniously expelled from.

The Othering

TIME SEEMED TO STRETCH INDEFINITELY WITHIN the dim confines of their shared captivity. The ceaseless incantations had long dissipated, leaving the cavernous temple cloaked in silence. The sun, weary from its celestial journey, gradually descended, casting sublime hues across the sky as dusk beckoned.

In this desolate chamber, the droplets found themselves divided, separated by an insidious undercurrent of prejudice. The Whites and the Translucents regarded each other with wary glances, their forced integration overshadowed by an unspoken animosity. Boond, however, refused to succumb to this division. Three times he reached out, his words woven with empathy, attempting to bridge the divide between the two factions. Yet, his gestures were met with cold indifference, faces frozen, and lips sealed in silent resistance. Even Sip, Raina, and Misty regarded him with bewildered eyes, their trust in him wavering.

Within the hollows of their confinement, the droplets sought solace within their own circles, forming miniature worlds of familiarity. Despite being packed together, they avoided each other, creating chasms of distrust that further deepened their weariness. Boond, burdened by the weight of their isolation, felt a profound sorrow welling within him.

As twilight descended, a creaking door shattered the stillness, heralding Pontiffa's arrival. The towering figure lifted the lotah with purpose, its contents clinking softly, and carried it outside into the fading light. In a solemn act, Pontiffa emptied the lotah, releasing the droplets into a rose bed that lined the nearby street.

Bonds
of Rescue

LIKE SHATTERED GLASS HURLED TO THE ground, the droplets collided with the scorching soil, their bodies ricocheting and splattering in an all directions. Helplessly, they careened and tumbled in every direction, uncontrollable fate deciding each droplets resting place. In this chaotic ballet of pain and disarray, their voices were silenced, their paths disrupted, as they struggled to find stability amidst the tumultuous landscape.

Amidst this dire scene, Boond and his steadfast companions clung to one another, their hands intertwined, and found themselves perched upon a brick ledge. On one side lay the flower bed, while on the other, a repugnant drain carried a thick, viscous slurry, teetering between solid and liquid states.

Horror seized their hearts as they peered down upon the flower bed. Thousands of droplets withered and vanished beneath the soil's hot surface in front of their eyes, swallowed by the hungry abyss. At the edge of the brick wall, two Whites struggled, desperately trying to evade the consuming grip of the desiccated earth. Without hesitation, Boond, with Raina tightly connected on one end, leaped from the wall. He stretched out his form, beckoning the nearest white stranger to take hold. "Grab me!" he cried out, urging them to join the desperate chain of survival. At first, the white stranger hesitated, only to have Boond whisper fiercely, "Do it! Unless you want to die." With a tentative reach, the large milky stranger finally attached himself to Boond, pulling the neighboring White along. Thus, they formed a lifeline, a lifeline of unity. Sip and Misty attached themselves to Raina, and together, with all the strength they could muster, they strained every ounce of their being, gradually hauling Boond and the two white strangers back to the safety of the scorching brick ledge. Exhausted and breathless, they collapsed upon its fiery surface.

As the intense heat bore down upon their rapidly shriveling bodies, they knew they had to press onward. In a demonstration of unwavering support, the six droplets linked themselves, assisting and encouraging one another as they inched toward the opposite side of the brick ledge. The distance felt like an eternity, fraught with treacherous terrain, porous and undulating, harboring deep craters that threatened to ensnare them in an eternal embrace of doom.

Finally, they reached the precipice, greeted by a noxious stench that made their insides churn. The thought of plunging into the murky gray abyss filled them with dread and revulsion. Yet, they realized they had no choice. The two Whites plunged first, their alabaster forms standing out starkly against the dismal sludge.

As Boond and his loyal friends prepared to take their own leap, they heard Misty's voice tremble with recognition. "Ripple? Ripple? Is that you?"

Their movements halted abruptly as they turned to follow Misty's gaze. There, before them, stood a frail, emaciated figure, resembling a desiccated prune, barely clinging to life. Yet, through the exhaustion and near-comatose state, a flicker of recognition illuminated his sunken eyes. Their spirits soared. They rushed to his side, their hearts brimming with both unalloyed joy and urgency. With gentle care, they cradled Ripple's diminished form, his weight almost imperceptible. Without a moment's hesitation, they turned toward the edge and, united by purpose, plunged headlong into the heavy embrace of the odorous sludge, mere inches away from the two white strangers.

The Dance
of Fate

As the droplets immersed themselves in the nourishing sludge, a miraculous transformation began to unfold. Ripple, in particular, underwent a breathtaking metamorphosis, drinking greedily from the thick substance. His once shriveled form plumped up, restoring him to the handsome, vibrant Ripple they had cherished in their memories. Overwhelmed with joy, the friends embraced and danced, momentarily forgetting the squalor of their surroundings.

Moved by the friends' selfless act of rescue, the two Whites approached with profound gratitude. "Sir, your kindness, openness, and generosity have humbled us," Doodh expressed, eyes focused on Boond, his voice filled with admiration. "Despite our initial closed-mindedness, suspicion, and prejudice, you reached out to us, and without hesitation, risked your life to save ours. We are forever indebted to you. My name is Doodh, and this is my sister, Lactosia."

Boond, embodying a self-effacing elegance and generous spirit, embraced them both warmly. The five friends introduced themselves, marking the beginning of a new, expanded friendship and the dismantling of mental prejudices and barriers. Slowly, almost as if they were moving through treacle, they made their way down the mountain slope, in the direction of the distant but delightfully familiar murmur of the mighty Sutlej.

Time seemed to stretch endlessly as Ripple shared his arduous journey since their separation, recounting tales of loneliness, heartbreak, beautiful sunrises, new friendships, capture, and abhishek.

They all listened in captivated silence, their hearts filled with empathy and admiration.

Ripple's voice trembled as he spoke of his final day.

The forceful collision with a rose bush had hurled him to the base of the towering brick wall, to which he clung with sheer grit, until he could muster the strength to start the climb. It took him half the night before he finally reached the top, his exhausted body yearning for rest, his very being on fire, surfaces raw from trying to hold on to the rough wall. He slept for hours, oblivious to the world, until the first rays of sunlight broke through, the warmth starting to build rapidly. Stirring from his slumber, his body aching and the heat intensifying, Ripple knew he had to move swiftly before the surface became too hot to bear. Summoning every ounce of remaining strength, he began to crawl, inch by agonizing inch, towards the edge. However, his body, drained of energy, gave in to exhaustion just inches from the end. Twenty fours had passed since he had been thrown from the urn, and it was in this desperate state that his beloved companions found and rescued him, their arrival a testament to the benevolent smile of Goddess Fortuna.

The friends listened intently, holding one another, marveling at the enigmatic workings of fate.

What if Ripple had reached the end?

Would they have ever reunited?

Filled with gratitude and surrender to forces beyond their control, they continued their journey, content and enveloped in the bonds of their newfound circle. Though the stench clung to them, it mattered not, for their spirits soared with joy.

The Receptacles of Waste

...SO SLOW WAS THEIR PROGRESS THAT it was early evening when the seven friends finally entered the village, only to be confronted with a stark transformation. What had been a yucky but peaceful journey turned into a malodorous ordeal as they found themselves subjected to continuous torrents of foul-smelling waste pouring out from the homes lining the drain. Recoiling in disgust, their senses and bodies assaulted by random putrid flows of refuse and waste, they faced an additional layer of degradation—the callous disregard of their existence.

As if from nowhere, Pontiffa's familiar face suddenly loomed large over them. Without a thought, he let out a spew of red beetle nut infused spittle that fell unceremoniously into the drain, its target nothing more than a mere receptacle for his disregard.

Like a gooey projectile, the thick mucus splattered over the seven friends, smothering them in a suffocating stringy ooze. Fighting for precious breath, the droplets convulsed in a frenzied dance, their futile struggles against the viscous tentacles of filth only entangling them further. Each desperate attempt to break free from the slimy grip was replaced by an onslaught of repugnant debris, seemingly the very essence of decay that was determined to suffocate their spirits. The world itself seemed to constrict around them, as if they had unwittingly stumbled upon the gates of Hades, enveloped in a nightmarish realm. Time stretched to a torturous crawl, as the unrelenting deluge pressed on unabated, assaulting their senses and testing their endurance.

But then, in a moment of deliverance, they left the wretched village behind, the cacophony of filth slowly fading into the distance.

The sound of the Sutlej grew louder, a comforting melody guiding them towards salvation. And just when it seemed they could endure no more, a sudden right turn revealed a breathtaking sight—clean, bubbling waters and the swift, dancing currents of the river a mere few feet away. Summoning their remaining strength, the friends propelled themselves through the putrid sludge, their determination growing with each stroke. Faster and faster, they swam, their movements fueled by a desperate yearning for the rejuvenating embrace of the river's fresh, tinkling, and cleansing waters.

A Translucent Metamorphosis

AS THEY CASCADED OVER THE EDGE, a reverberation of joyous cries filled the air, their bodies contorting with unrestrained delight, surrendering to the exhilarating embrace of the icy cold pristine waters. With each splash and somersault, the accumulated grime and filth were washed away, leaving them refreshed and renewed.

In the midst of their playful revelry, everyone's eyes started fixating on Doodh and Lactosia, witnessing a miraculous transformation unfold before their eyes. Within mere moments, the veil of whiteness dissipated, giving way to a beguiling translucency similar to all their friends.

Even Doodh and Lactosia themselves were awestruck by their newfound ethereal transformation. It was as if the Sutlej had stripped them of any superficial differentiation, making them all one.

Bathed in the golden sunlight, their translucent forms glistening like speckled gods, they stood as embodiments of grace and perfection. Their flawless proportions and elegant limbs stood in stark contrast to the other droplets, who appeared almost diminutive in comparison. Sip, unable to tear her eyes away from Doodh, felt an overwhelming gush blossoming within her—a love that transcended the boundaries of their liquid existence.

Boond's Contemplation

BOOND, IN THE MIDST OF HIS friends' joyful frolicking and newfound freedom, found himself swimming alone, his naturally introspective nature taking hold. A multitude of questions swirled within him, leaving him perplexed and deeply confused.

Nothing seemed to make sense.

How could it be that he and his fellow droplets, revered as instruments of purification in the morning, as they were poured on deities after morning prayers, ended up despised as nothing more than filth and slime mere hours later?

Exact same essence, yet defined, perceived and judged so differently.

How was it that all of us droplets, essentially the same in every respect, chose to distrust and dislike one another based solely on superficial appearance? What was even more perplexing was to witness this separation persisting, despite the fact that we were all facing the same uncertain fate. Our bias only adding to our collective distress, causing further angst, anguish, and exhaustion, as we maneuvered and struggled to avoid even the slightest touch. Why was this division and aversion so natural to us?

And so, Boond delved into contemplation, pondering the superficiality of judgment, the acts of labeling and othering. He reflected on the roots of hate, prejudice, and fear, contrasting them with the virtues of openness, kindness, and empathy. In his quest for understanding, Boond began to gain insights, unraveling the intricate threads that wove through the very fabric of existence.

The Pursuit
of Perfection

AS THE FRIENDS CONTINUED THEIR DESCENT from the majestic snow-capped Himalayas, their hearts brimming with joy and their bonds of friendship growing stronger, they marveled at the gradually flattening landscape. Vast meadows spread out in every direction, stretching as far as the eye could see, painting a picturesque panorama before them.

Each morning, while the rest of the droplets admired Sip's unwavering dedication, she would embark on a solitary journey of self-improvement. Driven by an insatiable desire to become the epitome of a sky-droplet, she pushed herself to the limits, enduring pain that seared through her very core.

Despite her near fatal encounter earlier, Sip was unwilling to relinquish her dream, her life's purpose. Surrendering to mediocrity was not an option, for it would render her existence nothing more than a hollow shell.

Sip had a simple motto in life. Never Give In.

She questioned how she could propel herself out of the water just a little faster. She pondered ways to widen her pancake shape, enabling her to stay suspended in the air for precious moments longer. She sought to extend her position, holding it for that millisecond more before gracefully piercing the fast-flowing river without a splash, marking the culmination of her flight.

The pursuit of absolute excellence in the realm of sky-droplets earned Sip admiration from both friends and strangers. No droplet had ever witnessed such perfection, span, and grace as she displayed.

She embodied the agility of a gymnast, the soaring grace of an eagle, and the precision of an Olympian diver, captivating all who beheld her remarkable talents.

While Doodh and Lactosia gradually grew accustomed to the attention and admiring looks from other droplets, initially feeling a tinge of self-consciousness, they eventually embraced their role as constant features in the lives of those around them. The five friends playfully teased them, affectionately nicknaming them Shiva and Lakshmi in recognition of their god-like stature.

Yet, amidst the never-ending tribute of admiration, Doodh became increasingly oblivious to the external world. His focus narrowed, and his attention fixated on Sip alone. He cherished the moments when she immersed herself in practice, marveling at her sheer persistence. He delighted in her presence, when she joined the gang exhausted but content. And his eyes would follow her steadily receding form, bidding her farewell early each night as she prepared for the demanding schedule that awaited her the next morning.

The
Fading Joy

MANY MOONS HAD PASSED SINCE THEIR journey began, and the vibrant mountain meadows had transformed into the dusty plains of the Punjab. The river flowed with a comforting warmth, and their once sprightly voyage had settled into relative serenity.

Amidst great pomp and splendor, Doodh and Sip had celebrated their union, their love elevated and idolized. They became the revered couple, the first family, while thousands of droplets cheered and reveled in their anointed royalty.

However, as time passed, Sip underwent a profound change. Fame and adoration had permeated her being, seeping deep into her psyche. Where once she found joy and purpose in striving, in reaching unparalleled heights, now her driving force was reduced to an unquenchable thirst for adulation, adoration, and attention.

Boond, Ripple, Misty, Raina, and even the stunning Lactosia became insignificant in her eyes. She acknowledged them with a mere nod, devoid of love or connection. While the friends remained close, engaging in nightly revelries and animated conversations, an unspoken sadness lingered, overshadowed by Sip's absence.

Day by day, her transformation grew more pronounced. The inner joy and vitality that once defined her were reduced to a hollow memory. She became perpetually craving, in constant need of acknowledgment, an emotional beggar whose well-being depended on an insatiable hunger for recognition and worship. Fragile, fearful, and desperate, she constantly yearned for the spotlight.

Simultaneously, her once sleek and bright form succumbed to the weight of opulence, becoming bloated, plump and murky – a physical manifestation of her emotional state.

The
Ascendance

AND THEN, THE INEVITABLE HAPPENED. SURAJ – that source of light and warmth – had just barely peeked over the eastern horizon. Shadows still a mile long. Chutki, a newcomer who had landed among them as a drop of monsoon joy just a few weeks ago, was spellbound by Sip's presence from the moment she joined them. It was all she wanted to do.

To become.

Her hero – Sip the legend.

Like Sip, Chutki lived for one thing. And one thing only. To become the greatest sky-droplet ever. She worked, she struggled, she endured pain, she persevered, she experienced failure.

But it was all she lived for. The joy, the exhilaration. The dance towards perfection.

Chutki, with all her heart and an indescribable depth of focus, accelerated. Every bit of her driven to the point of fatigue. Her trajectory aimed directly at the orange orb rising just over the horizon. Like a heavenly angel, she took flight – up, up, up.

Higher.

Longer.

An arc that seemed to touch the very heavens. As everyone watched in awe and surrender, she hovered... and stayed. Before transforming into the tip of an arrow that sliced through the river's surface, without a single splash.

The thousands of droplets had just witnessed something unprecedented. A roar of applause – of adoration – arose as if from the very depths of the Sutlej. From its very core. Adoration intertwined with recognition... the ultimate sky-droplet had appeared. Oh! What a great fortune!

Sip... soft, needy, and fragile, felt the very essence of life dissipate from within her. Purpose lost. Empty. Hollow. A nobody. Life no longer held any meaning.

As Suraj rose to its zenith, its scorching heat making even the brown clay of the Punjab simmer with unbearable warmth, Sip, eyes closed, withdrawn, shattered... slowly floated to the surface. Liquid form outstretched, embracing as vast a canvas as possible. Absorbing. Transforming.

Until the gentle northwesterly gusts of Loo scooped her out of the waters. Tenderly cradling her in his dry, arid embrace. Like a fluttering kite, lifting her away. Into the heavens above.

Far, far away.

The Great Divide

As Boond and his friends continued their meandering journey through the scorching plains of Punjab, the Sutlej abruptly made a sharp turn to the right, revealing a truly awe-inspiring sight. The right bank of the river seemed to vanish into an expansive flow of water, dwarfing them in size by at least tenfold.

The merging of the teeming millions of the river Chenab overwhelmed them in every conceivable way. It felt as though a peaceful farming community had been transported to the edge of a metropolis, with its bustling frenzy, vibrant activity, and rapid exchanges. The experience was utterly overwhelming.

Initially, the friends found it exhilarating. Everyone appeared so sophisticated, cultured, and refined, making them feel like simpletons in comparison. However, beneath the surface glamour and sophistication, they couldn't help but notice a dark undercurrent that permeated the Chenabis.

The Chenabis were divided nearly evenly, with the Monal Chenabis distinguished by their blue markings and the Musk Chenabis by their unique insignia. Despite living and traveling together, an undeniable sense of suspicion and animosity existed between them. Covert attacks, open derision, and the formation of factions created an atmosphere charged with tension.

Barely had the two rivers completed their intermingling when Boond and his friends found themselves being pulled in conflicting directions. If in the morning, it would be the Monals, then in the evening, it would be the Musks fervently sharing their Great Story, Great Prophet, and Great God.

Again and again, the Monals and the Musks declared, "If you refuse to believe in what we offer, then you must understand that sooner or later, you will reach the Great Ocean. There, your life will be filled with torment and suffering. This is your chance to join us, the true believers. By doing so, not only will you be protected on our journey together, but for eternity itself."

The friends felt an increasing unease as they witnessed this divisive rhetoric. Parallels between the Chenabis' feuds and the conflicts they had observed at the temple began to emerge. The sense of exclusivity claims of superiority, and fear of the other had created whirlpools of hatred and misunderstandings.

Boond, with his budding wisdom, started questioning the validity of such divisions. What were the stories behind them? And why this need to have a monopoly over the One and Only Truth?

Driven by his thirst for understanding, Boond engaged in conversations with dozens of Chenabis. Only to find himself being proselytized and lectured to, leaving him disheartened. Just when hope was fading, Boond's attention was captured by a wizened old drop who bore no markings and traveled alone—an anomaly among the other Chenabis. Boond felt an undeniable pull towards this figure, hoping against hope that he might finally learn the history of the Chenabis.

"It is a long story, my son," whispered the emaciated figure with the kindest eyes Boond had ever seen. "If you are willing to listen, then come, let us travel together for a while."

Friend. Mentor.
Guide.

FOR MANY DAYS AND NIGHTS, AS the moon waxed and waned, Boond found himself captivated by his newfound friend. Abi, full of wisdom and knowledge, became more than a companion; she evolved into a mentor, guide, and the Teacher of Histories.

Under Abi's tutelage, Boond's education thrived. He discovered the art of scavenging for sustenance in the sandy crevices that adorned the riverbank. Abi's seemingly magical ability to conjure nourishment from thin air fascinated him. She consumed only the barest minimum to sustain herself, generously sharing the rest with those less fortunate. Patiently, she revealed the secrets of discerning edible morsels from potential dangers.

Diving deep became another skill under Boond's belt. Abi taught him the delicate art of equalizing internal and external pressures, allowing them to explore the river's bottom without fear of being crushed. In the depths, where others might have faltered, Boond discovered a new sense of purpose.

However, it wasn't only physical skills that Abi imparted. Through her, Boond delved into the art of quiet contemplation. They would sit suspended in the river's depths, surrounded by the hushed rush of water above them. Guided by Abi's calming presence, Boond ventured deeper within himself, uncovering the uncharted realms of his consciousness. Abi's wisdom and love served as a compass, guiding his inner exploration.

As they swam, learned, and shared stories, Abi shared tales of ancient mythology—the Chenabis, stretching back to the dawn of time. She painted vivid pictures of their origins, their journey through history, and the reasons underlying their present strife. Boond listened with rapt attention, the history of the Chenabis becoming a treasure trove of knowledge within his expanding consciousness.

Spellbound Encounters and Divine Smells

"LONG LONG AGO, LOST IN THE *mists of time, a delicate snowflake grace-fully descended into a breathtaking alpine valley. The vista before her was a sight to behold—towering snow-capped peaks embraced the valley, while*

pristine lakes reflected the azure sky. The air was crisp, carrying a hint of pine and the freshness of untouched nature.

As gentle winds swirled around, the snowflake's attention was captivated by a magnificent stag standing tall amidst the grandeur. Its powerful body was adorned with massive, perfectly shaped antlers that seemed to touch the heavens. Mesmerized, the snowflake yearned to get closer to this splendid creature. As if her prayers were answered, a whisper of a gust lifted her up, placing her delicately on the deer's sinewy haunches.

The deer's radiating warmth embraced the snowflake, causing her to melt and merge into a perfect liquid orb. The captivating musky scent emanating from the celestial being permeated her essence, seeping into her very core.

In a trance-like state, she slid off the deer's glistening fur, falling onto the cold snow below. Once again frozen, but unlike her neighboring snowflakes, she had been touched by a divine encounter. Emitting a bewitching aura, she captivated all those around her, leaving them enthralled.

As layers of snow covered them, Sava, the snowflake, shared her mystical experience with a captivated audience. Slowly, like the other snowflakes, they all entered a deep slumber. However, Sava and her companions had vivid dreams and visions of The Great Musk—the source of everything. Their deepest longing was to find a way back to Him, guided by Sava's profound revelation.

Sava's captivating and vivid description of the love and ecstasy she had experienced in The Great Musk's presence illuminated the purpose of life itself. It was to reside eternally in His divine presence, where every day would be filled with pure joy and exhilaration, an everlasting bliss.

With compassion and generosity, Sava outlined the path that each droplet must follow, revealing the right mindset and actions required to reach Him. Her chosen descent allowed her to share the Secret Path with others, guiding them towards the ultimate destination.

Gratitude and visions filled the dreams of her slumbering companions. Meanwhile, Sava remained in a deep trance, reliving her memories and united with The Great Musk. The subtle perfume diffusing from within her made each moment a vivid reality, a manifestation of the profound connection she had forged."

The Ultimate
Vision

"*Even as Sava had just begun to share her story with her newfound admirers, barely two valleys further, Nita was descending from the last remnants of clouds. The sky above was a brilliant blue, bathed in the radiant rays of Suraj. The air at this rare altitude was thin and pure, causing*

the world around her to shimmer with a sparkling allure. Sunlight danced off the pristine white snow, illuminating the dark green shrubs and the brackish brown and black boulders peeking through the blanket of white.

Nita's senses were overwhelmed by the breathtaking beauty of her surroundings. And then, she saw her—the most resplendent and vibrant being she had ever encountered. It was as if the heavens had opened up to present her with the ultimate gift.

This noble creature walked gracefully across the pure white canvas, emanating a spellbinding display of colors and hues that Nita had never witnessed before. Brilliant blues seamlessly merged with verdant greens, purples, and reds. Adorning its regal head sat a dazzling crest of emerald green, akin to the crown of divinity itself. Encircling its captivating and benevolent dark eyes, which seemed to penetrate Nita's very soul, were rings of iridescent blue.

As Nita gazed into those eyes, she felt an undeniable pull, as though being drawn into a vortex of knowledge and love. The illusion of a deep black center, encircled by a halo of radiant blue, intensified the sensation, as if she were receiving revelations through a portal connecting to another realm.

Who was this magnificent being? Nita yearned to know, feeling deep within her that this encounter held profound significance. She sensed that this was the Final Vision, an experience that would leave no questions unanswered.

"Who? Who?" Nita's mind screamed, the longing for knowledge echoing through her. And then, from the depths of the universe, she heard the faintest whisper on the wind, barely audible yet carrying immense meaning. "This, dear Nita, is the Great Monal."

In that moment, Nita's mind found peace. She knew. She understood. Every truth she needed to grasp was revealed to her.

Filled with gratitude and love, Nita felt an innate urge to share and guide others. And so she did. As they fell into deep slumber, the blessed *followers of the Great Monal formed a circle of connection around Nita, enveloped in reverence and devotion.*

The original disciples.
The Chosen.
The Monals."

Unity and Dissent:
the Flow of Belief

"*THE SPRING THAW ENVELOPED THE VAST expanse of the Himalayas, witnessing an incredible transformation as countless snowflakes metamorphosed into droplets. They embarked on a collective journey, joining forces as rivulets that swelled into brooks, merging with one another to form streams, finally to combine into mighty rivers.*

For days on end, Nita and her devoted followers cascaded downward like a bubbling, gurgling brook. As new droplets joined their harmonious descent, Nita or one of her growing number of disciples would impart teachings about the Great Monal and the profound purpose of life. Enthralled and captivated, the majority embraced this faith wholeheartedly, proudly adorning their foreheads with the mystical blue insignia, just like their revered elders.

They felt a sense of belonging. They were Monals.

However, there remained a small, peculiar minority among them. These individuals insisted on relying solely on their own experiences. Whether subtly or more directly, they made it clear that they were uninterested in embracing someone else's story, no matter how sincere or lovingly shared. To them, it was merely a tale, not their own.

Consequently, they found themselves as outcasts—a tiny, marginalized few viewed with suspicion. The weight of ostracization pressed upon them, and as each day passed, a few would succumb to the allure of conformity. It was easier to embrace the Acceptance, don the blue insignia, and find a sense of belonging once again. Gradually, their numbers dwindled until unmarked droplets on their individual paths were a rarity. Content to march to their own inner rhythm, these unique individuals seemed at peace in solitude. Even when chance encounters brought them together, a few heartfelt conversations sufficed before they resumed their separate journeys.

And so the ever-expanding river of blue continued its inexorable descent. Gurgling and flowing, it grew into an expanding family of interconnected believers, united by a shared understanding of purpose and destination. With their swelling numbers came the development of rituals, morality, laws, and beliefs—complex and nuanced, mirroring the intricacies of their growing community."

Colliding Currents:
the Clash of Beliefs

"THE MEMORY OF THAT FATEFUL DAY *remained etched in Nita's mind and the hearts of her disciples. The day that changed everything.*

Thirteen days and nights of travel had brought them together, their pool of believers growing harmoniously. Love, knowledge, and sharing were the tools they used to imprint their truth on open, receptive minds, like blank slates waiting to be filled.

It was late afternoon when a distant roar first caught their attention. Initially faint, beyond the towering mountain range on their left, the sound grew louder with each passing hour. Then, without warning, the silhouette of the mountain dissolved rapidly, as two tributaries merged in a tumultuous clash of swirling eddies and disarrayed whirlpools.

The Monals stood shocked and surprised, overwhelmed by the sheer number of new droplets they had merged with. Never before had they encountered such a vast congregation. But to their dismay, these strangers possessed their own messiah, their own stories, gods, and rituals. They were unwilling to embrace the teachings of the True Prophet or the path to eternal presence in the Great Monal's realm. Instead, they propagated blasphemy, praying to some false god and engaging in strange rituals. To make matters worse, they adorned themselves with a strange, grotesque insignia.

Confusion and bewilderment transformed into a seething anger. These individuals were truly lost, obstinately blind to the guiding light. Their disagreements escalated into violent clashes even as they navigated treacherous gorges, crashing against unforgiving rocks and succumbing to the torrents of uncontrollable rapids. Even the tranquil alpine meadows failed to subdue the unending turmoil that plagued the now mighty river.

Thus, the Chenab flowed, its inhabitants consumed by self-righteousness and enduring distrust. Everyone's eyes remained ever watchful, eagerly seizing each new droplet that entered their realm before the other side could claim them. They clung steadfastly to their beliefs, unyielding in their conviction of their own truth and the falsehoods of the others. Their mission: to save the souls of newcomers, shielding them from the treacherous grip of delusion and falsehood.

From that day onwards, peace became but a distant memory.

However, a few droplets remained unmarked, belonging to no group. These solitary souls, physically emaciated from their life on the outskirts, bore the weight of their outcast status. Their liquid forms were feeble, stripped of the vibrant hues that adorned their counterparts. They carried the scars of rejection, their once-pristine orbs marked by the harshness of their existence. But amidst their frailty, they persevered, unwavering in their commitment to their inner truths. Living on the fringes of society, they eschewed conformity, refusing to be swayed by the judgment and hatred that surrounded them."

The Path
of Solitude

"AND THERE, MY SON, YOU HAVE it. I have taught you everything I know. Shared with you all the knowledge I have gathered," Abi smiled, reaching out to embrace Boond with a tender, lingering hug. "Now, the time has come for me to continue on my personal quest."

"Boond, you must decide who you are. Who you want to be. Choose very carefully, for it is only your life that hangs in the balance," Abi chuckled, relishing her own wry humor, before disappearing into the depths of the dark waters.

Boond's heart sank with a heavy weight of desolation. Over the course of their journey together, Abi had become someone special to him. Wise, kind, and filled with knowledge, she radiated warmth and love that had touched Boond to his very core. He felt a profound sadness as he watched her depart.

Now, Boond was truly, unequivocally alone. The once unbreakable circle of friendship that had sustained and nourished him from the moment he evaporated from the Great Ocean had shattered into countless pieces. Ripple, Raina, and Lactosia had embraced the path of the Monals, while Misty and Doodh had become fervent Musks. Hatred simmered between the two factions, evident in their reproachful, suspicious glances whenever they crossed paths. It was only for old time's sake that they never resorted to physical altercations.

But for all his former companions, Boond was truly the object of their deepest contempt. The others, deluded as they were, at least deserved respect. They were Believers. Boond, in their collective eyes, was nothing more than scum, a polluted and filthy outcast they wished to never lay eyes upon again.

Boond understood. He accepted.

His decision became crystal clear—he would embrace solitude. He would forge his own path, seeking the truth for himself. And in that space of surrender, he found his quietude and peace.

Another World

As had become his habit, Boond swam along the river's edge, seeking solace in nature. Here, far from the mocking voices and jeering crowds of the believers, he could immerse himself in the sensory onslaught of the hot, dry plains of the Punjab. As the afternoon sun beat down incessantly, the brown clay baked to a shimmering surface, causing the air itself to quiver and dance with the touch of invisible flames. Lost in contemplation, Boond's gaze fixated on distant objects, their forms seemingly writhing and swaying to an inner melody, as if the rising heat distorted and transformed them into fluid, living entities.

With each passing day, Boond's perception had sharpened, unveiling reality in its purest essence—devoid of interpretation, labels, or judgment. As he delved deeper into his inner world, an ever-expanding sense of connection and well-being bloomed within him. He felt a merging of his being with the distant tree, the arid soil, the grazing cows and goats, the green reeds gently swaying at the river's edge, and even the subtlest eddies and ripples where the water met protruding boulders. The boundaries of separation dissolved, and he became part of the grand symphony of existence—a harmonious flow of life.

In the midst of this profound metamorphosis, a peculiar sight caught Boond's attention—an enigmatic stagnant pool nestled along the river's edge. The pool was a surreal tableau, carved out of the riverbank with a circular rock berm enclosing it protectively. Its waters shimmered with an eerie, deep green hue, while a pungent stench of decaying vegetation permeated the air in a continuous, noxious stream.

Curiosity compelled Boond to swim closer, disregarding the repulsive odor that assailed his senses. As he approached, the pool revealed its secrets, unveiling a fascinating scene.

Thousands of shriveled droplets busied themselves within the stagnant pool, their movements purposeful and laborious. Oblivious to the vast expanse of the open, flowing river just beyond the rock edge, they toiled within the confines of their murky sanctuary. Intrigued, Boond made a determined effort to overcome his initial recoil, gracefully maneuvering himself onto the broad rock shelf that barely breached the water's surface. And with a decisive plunge, he descended into the turbid depths, his senses enveloped by the strange and mysterious world that awaited him.

Time seemed suspended as Boond found himself surrounded by a sea of gaunt, emaciated faces. Their eyes wide in disbelief, their expressions mirroring their incredulous astonishment at the arrival of an unexpected visitor.

Privilege
and the Price

"Ahem!" The sound of a loud throat clearing from a rock shelf above, on the river's edge broke the spell. "Come, swim over to me and let these folk get back to their work."

As if electrified, all the droplets dispersed, scurrying back to their strange tasks that Boond had never encountered before.

Curiosity piqued, Boond swam toward the ledge, observing the scene before him. He found a shallow bath of warm, still water occupied by a small group of plump well-nourished droplets. The absence of flowing water had transformed the pool into a sun-soaked hot tub. Surrounding the lounging droplets were many shriveled droplets engaged in various tasks. Some meticulously removed any stray plant fibers, while others applied a vibrant purple paste to the bodies of the loungers. A third group diligently adjusted broad leaves, acting as umbrellas to shield the sun's direct rays.

The sight was surreal—an existence without flow, a battle against nature's course, sustained at the expense of weary and fatigued droplets.

Boond's attention was drawn to the corpulent few, their surfaces stretched to parchment, threatening to burst at any moment. What startled him most was the vivid purple paste covering every inch of their bulging forms. Should even the tiniest portion peel away, one of the workers would swiftly cover the exposed area. The perfect purple ovals remained intact—on the verge of bursting.

"Stranger, what is your name?" The rotund droplet that had beckoned Boond over asked.

"Boond."

"What brings you here?"

"Curiosity, really."

"We didn't even think it was possible for your kind to climb into our world."

"I hope that is OK?"

"Oh of course! We have only heard stories about you, passed down from our ancestors. You see, we have lived in this kingdom of Khuk for thousands of generations. The Great Legend warns us of the terrible dangers of leaving this sanctuary and dropping into the flow. The strange beasts that swallow you. Or getting sprayed on to the dry riverbank, only to have your life sucked out of you as the hot soil devours you like quicksand. Or disappearing into the beak of a diving hawk... or... terrible, terrible, terrible. It just goes on and on and on.

But I talk too much! You are here, in flesh and blood. Finally, we will learn about life out in the flow. Come. Sit. Share your story and your journey. Make yourself comfortable. Here, eat these mulberries. The chelas work day and night to tend and grow and pluck them for us."

And so, Boond obliged, surrounded by diligent workers who catered to his every need. Ravenous and emaciated himself, Boond indulged in the plump droplets' offerings, a mix of comfort and guilt stirring within him. He felt his heart bleed for these exhausted overworked droplets – what were they called? Chelas? – as they toiled ceaselessly to provide luxury for his enjoyment.

For a while, Boond surrendered to the hedonistic pleasures, savoring the berries and the attention, while sharing tales of the outside world. The droplets listened in awe, having never encountered the majesty of the Himalayas, with their snowcapped peaks or lush green verdant valleys saturated in fragrant flowers. They were surprised to learn that they were capable of freezing solid only to melt back again.

With each revelation, new questions arose, and Boond patiently answered them, painting vivid landscapes and diverse beings in their minds.

Days turned into weeks, and Boond grew plumper, indulging in the comforts of his surroundings. Sedentary and lethargic, he reveled in the attention and the sharing of knowledge. Until finally, all questions were answered, and the curiosity of the droplets seemed satiated.

"Now, it is my turn." Boond looked at his host. "I am filled with curiosity. Never have I seen a society structured like this. And this paste! What is the obsession with staying covered all the time? What is it made of and who makes it? I have a hundred questions on my mind."

The
Sacred Way

BOND LISTENED, LEARNED AND ABSORBED.

For countless generations, the Khuks had thrived in their secluded pond, tracing their origins back to the Original Storm that had flooded the plains of Punjab for three days and three nights. The Great Legend recounted the celestial descent of the Osmoses, revered as incarnates of the gods, who chose this sanctuary as their divine abode.

Within the protected lagoon, an imposing Mulberry Goddess tree towered on its edge, providing shelter and an abundant supply of succulent fruit to satisfy the Osmoses' desires. Broad leaves fell from the tree, diligently collected by the Chelas, to create a canopy of shade during the scorching summer months, ensuring the Osmoses' comfort.

The pond's surface bloomed with vibrant purple Hyacinths, meticulously tended by the Chelas. These delicate flowers required constant care, pruning, and plucking. The petals were carried upstream to the pebble factory, where skilled Chelas transformed them into a thick paste. This paste, crushed and ground, would be applied to the opulent Osmoses, adorning them in their distinctive purple hue.

In the early days, the over-fed Osmoses would occasionally explode without warning, leaving the surrounding droplets in shock and dismay. This phenomenon created an atmosphere of anxiety and fear among the Osmoses, as they lived in constant anticipation of their own detonation.

The seventh chapter of the Great Legend told the story of the Divine Revelation which unfolded through the visionary dreams of Pita, a child prodigy. In his dreams, the gods unveiled the purpose of the local flowers, revealing their protective and transformative properties for the Osmoses. From that moment onward, no Osmoses would ever explode again, and the distinction between the purple clad opulent Osmoses and the dedicated Chelas became forevermore stark.

The gods, in their infinite wisdom and benevolence, ensured a continuous supply of new Chelas, showering them from the heavens during every monsoon. These fresh innocent droplets revitalized the exhausted ranks, replenishing the spent, emaciated Chelas who would silently wither away during the scorching summer afternoons.

This intricate harmony and purpose resonated throughout the Khuk civilization, elucidated in the Great Legend as The Way. Every droplet had its role to play, aligned with the cosmic order. By adhering to this sacred Way, the world would spin harmoniously on its axis. Because the Osmoses were protected and cared for, the gods in heaven would be pleased. And because they were pleased, they in turn would bestow their blessings upon the kingdom of Khuk, perpetuating the virtuous cycle of abundance and protection.

The Night of Reflection and Escape

THE SUN WAS SLOWLY SINKING OVER the western horizon, casting elongated shadows of the Mulberry Goddess clear across the mighty Chenab. Young Chelas, who had spent most of the day arranging leaves to shield the Osmoses from the scorching sun, were now busy removing the wilted umbrellas from the water's surface. Tomorrow's breeze would bring a fresh supply of plump, broad leaves, ready to provide shade for the Osmoses once more.As the day turned to dusk, many Osmoses retired for the night. The Chelas applying a final thick layer of purple paste as insurance until the morning check-up, nine hours away.

Boond coughed, his corpulent body jiggling like unsettled jelly on a damaged conveyor belt. Lately, he found himself wheezing frequently, the pressure from his engorged form squeezing his organs in a constant vice. He felt a searing pain run through his envelope of skin. That pressure from his last cough seemed to pull his already stretched skin to its very limit. Boond looked down at his swollen stomach as it pulsated shallowly, in unison with his labored breathing.

Fear and disgust gripped Boond's heart as he heard Abi's words echoing within him. "Boond, you must decide who you are, who you want to be. Choose very carefully, for it is only your life that hangs in the balance."

It was a moonless night, and darkness enveloped the lagoon. The only sounds were the soft wheezing and loud snores of the senescent Osmoses. Silently, Boond waded to the ledge's edge, trying not to disturb the exhausted Chelas, slumped uncomfortably over whatever provided their broken bodies a modicum of comfort. With an uncomfortably loud splash, he dropped his jiggling body into the big pond. Fearful that he might have awoken the Chelas, he held his breath, remaining as still as possible. Thankfully, the slumbering droplets remained oblivious to his presence, lost in their own restless sleep, knowing that back-breaking work awaited them in a few hours.

Carefully maneuvering through the masses, Boond finally reached the rock edge. With great effort, he heaved himself onto the shelf and dragged his rotund form to the other side. Without looking back, he splashed into the cool flowing waters of the Chenab, leaving behind the stagnant pool and the life he had known for multiple seasons, with its relentless cycle of excess and indulgence. The rushing river embraced him, carrying him away into the night.

Embracing Purpose
Amidst Scarcity

MANY MOONS HAD PASSED SINCE BOOND'S escape from the stagnant pool. Though not gaunt like before, his once corpulent form had transformed into a wiry frame, enabling him to swim strongly along the river's edge. Food was scarce, and Boond often had to dive deep into the river's depths to scrounge for scraps, where he would encounter other emaciated Unmarked droplets.

Despite his own hunger, Boond's heart overflowed with compassion and love. Without hesitation, he would share the majority of whatever meager findings he had, reserving only a few crumbs for himself. As he looked into the eyes of the grateful recipients, who were often strangers he would likely never see again, he found profound purpose in providing nourishment and connection to fellow beings.

Hours were spent diving deep within himself, tapping into the inner well of contentment and spiritual abundance. In those moments, Boond allowed the river's currents to guide him passively, embracing the flow of life. Interspersed with his wakeful scavenging for food, he found connection and compassion in each encounter.

Boond's existence had taken on a new meaning. No longer driven by hedonism, he had transcended his former self. Shame had given way to gratitude for the lessons it had taught him. Every touch, every shared moment, every act of kindness and love, no matter how small, became a declaration of the profound purpose that had awakened within him. In the face of scarcity, Boond found richness in giving, and in that richness, he was fulfilled beyond measure.

The Burden
of Accumulation

As Boond's inner transformation continued to deepen, he found himself observing things just as they were.

Without judgment.

Without labels.

Speaking very little, he developed a sense of clarity that allowed him to see the world with newfound depth.

He was developing the ability to remain in Awareness.

Heading south through Sindh, leaving the arid plains of Punjab behind, the air grew heavier with moisture as they approached the Arabian Sea. Traces of saltiness hit his nostrils. An inexplicable sense of familiarity and belonging stirred within Boond, guiding him like a gentle current. Though he couldn't fully articulate or remember the feeling, he trusted it as if it was leading him home.

He sensed it.

Yet, the journey had slowed to a crawl. No longer were they dancing and bubbling down the Himalayan mountains as free-flowing droplets. Boond watched the Monals and the Musks, still adorned with their bright insignias, but he observed the emptiness and ritualistic nature of their actions. Their fervor and commitment had faded, replaced by a ravenous pursuit of material amassment.

It had begun with a few droplets adorning themselves in the bright yellow pollen carried from the surrounding sunflower fields. Others, striving to outdo them, collected the vibrant effulgence emitted by the cotton dyeing mills along the riverbanks. Thus, engaged in an escalating contest of accumulation, they transformed into grotesque, swollen entities weighed down by baubles. Their insatiable greed and envy burdened them, hindering their movement within the current. Emotionally drained and physically encumbered, they trudged towards the vast expanse of the open sea, the once-mighty river now reduced to a sluggish, treacle-like flow.

The
Ocean's Embrace

As the river meandered towards its grand finale, the droplets, be they Monals, Musks, or the Unmarked, couldn't help but feel
terrified. Their journey had been long and arduous, filled with trans-
formations and revelations, yet none of them could have foreseen the
immense expanse that lay ahead – the vast, turbulent Ocean.

Approaching the shoreline, the droplets witnessed a spectacle of
awe-inspiring magnitude. Their elders just ahead of them, once proud
and pompous, now faced the relentless onslaught of the ocean's colossal

waves. Each surge of water engulfed millions, creating a swirling cauldron of frothy foam that seemed to devour their existence before receding, leaving the next batch at the forefront, ready to be devoured in turn.

Fear gripped the hearts of the approaching droplets. They saw their companions pulled away, naked and devoid of all their belongings – the attainments they had collected with such avarice and sacrificed so much to attain. With each wave's embrace, it was as if the ocean stripped them bare, leaving only their greed and unfulfilled desires as their remaining companions.

Despite their resistance and desperate struggle, the river's relentless force pushed them closer to the abyss. They were on the brink of facing the vast unknown, and terror loomed like an ominous cloud over their consciousness. What lay beyond this final journey? Was it the end, or just another beginning? The answers eluded them, hidden deep within the ocean's unfathomable depths.

They could sense the ocean's insatiable hunger, yearning to consume all that approached its shores. Yet, they also felt a peculiar, inexplicable pull, as if some cosmic force was drawing them towards it, pulling them into its enigmatic embrace.

The droplets knew that the ocean held its secrets, and as they dropped into its waters, they were swept away by currents beyond their comprehension. For a time, they bobbed in its vastness, amidst waves that seemed to cradle and caress them, while within their liquid forms, they felt a subtle yet profound transformation occurring.

In the ocean's realm, they discovered a sense of surrender – an acceptance of their fate and place in the grand scheme of existence. Their identities as individuals dissolved, and they became one with the ebb and flow of the ocean's tides.

Time in the ocean seemed ethereal, as if seconds merged with eternity. They felt the whispers of the wind and the embrace of the sun's warm rays. It was a paradoxical existence, neither here nor there, suspended in a realm where time and space intermingled.

Yet, the ocean knew its purpose. When the time was right, it would gently lift these droplets to the surface, where the bright sun would shine upon them once more. With the winds as their guide, they would be carried back to the Himalayas, beginning another cycle of life, death, and rebirth.

For eternity.

Homecoming

AS ALL THE OTHER DROPLETS CONTINUE their upward journey, bobbing around seemingly without freedom or agency, Boond takes a deep breath, summoning all his life-force within. With determined focus, he plunges towards the ocean depths, embracing darkness, stillness, peace, and tranquility. Deeper and deeper he goes, shutting out the fear that grips him,

propelled by an inexorable force, a deep premonition, and an inexplicable desire. It feels like destiny.

Down he descends, leaving the familiar world behind, surrounded by the chilling void of the ocean's abyss. The pressure builds, squeezing him tightly, but he perseveres, going further into the unknown, not knowing how much more he can endure.

In this uncharted realm, grotesque and eyeless creatures become his companions, and the cold engulfs him. Boond pushes on, driven by an inner calling, as if the very essence of his being seeks solace in this mysterious deep.

And then, like magic, it happens. A burst of effulgent aurelian-blue light envelops him, illuminating the darkness. In an instant, all pain, pressure, and fear vanish, replaced by a sense of weightlessness and freedom. Boond's form becomes luminescent, harmonizing with the glowing surroundings.

In this spiritual realm, he finds himself connected to millions of other droplets, all emanating the same brilliant sapphire-gold light. An overwhelming feeling of love surges within him, not directed towards another but flowing outwards towards all, embracing everything and everyone. As he merges with the collective consciousness, he realizes that he is both an individual and part of a boundless, non-dual unity.

Love washes over him, uniting him with the Source, the Infinite. Time loses its meaning, and Boond transcends the limits of physical existence. He experiences an expansion of his inner self, breaking free from the constraints of individuality.

In this cosmic union, he discovers profound knowledge and infinite love. He is home, lost in the timeless embrace of Om, the eternal sound of the universe.

With a heart brimming with joy, Boond knows he has broken free from the cycle of life, death, and rebirth. He has transcended the limitations of form and ego, realizing that he is an integral part of the interconnected whole.

He is Everything. He is Nothing.

Silence fills his being, and he basks in the bliss of Realization. Boond has found his quintessence, his eternal home. The journey is complete, and he is now free to dwell in the boundless expanse of existence, forever united with the cosmic dance of the universe.

Home.

Home.

Om...

EPILOGUE

IF YOU FOUND JOY AND INSPIRATION in this novella, I'd be grateful if you could share it with your friends or acquaintances.

And if this journey touched your heart and you feel inclined to give back to the Universe, here are a few charities that are making a significant impact, offering a helping hand to those in need.

An ocean, after all, is nothing but a collection of drops.

https://ffe.org/
https://foundation.fhda.edu/how-to-give/
https://aif.org/

Education is an investment with the power to yield infinite returns. Nurturing enlightened minds, honing critical thinking skills, leads to just, prosperous, and compassionate societies. The ripple effect of rescuing a child from dropping out extends far beyond our imagination.

https://awionline.org/

Just because a sentient being may not look like us, or be able to communicate the way we do, does not mean that they are incapable of suffering. Being kind and generous towards those that have agency and power is to be practical. To be kind and generous towards the weakest – that is to be noble.

https://icfaid.org/

Another way to help the most vulnerable amongst us – children. It's good to know that 99% of the funds actually reach the recipients.

None of these are interesting? Pick a cause or a group that touches your heart. Make the world a slightly better place and feel the joy.

ABOUT THE AUTHOR

BUNTER THE HIMALAYAN IS NOT MY 'real' name.

But yet, it is.

All through my boarding school years – six through sixteen – that was who I was. In college, that started to change. By the time I became a 'grown up', it had faded into the background.

Perfect. It points to me. But it is not really me.

What more can one ask for?

Vibrant Truth, instead of a pale description.